CONFESSIONS OF A CPA:
The Capital Equivalent Value of Life Insurance

BY

Bryan S. Bloom, CPA

INFINITY
PUBLISHING

Copyright © 2018 by Bryan S. Bloom, CPA

ISBN 978-1-49-583071-6

Published April 2018

INFINITY PUBLISHING
1094 New DeHaven Street, Suite 100
West Conshohocken, PA 19428-2713
Toll-free (877) BUY BOOK
Local Phone (610) 941-9999
Fax (610) 941-9959
Info@buybooksontheweb.com
www.buybooksontheweb.com

What Others Are Saying about Confessions of a CPA: The Truth About Life Insurance

This is the third book I've read on life insurance. Perhaps because of the knowledge I gained in the other two, or perhaps because of the way Bloom writes, I better understand these concepts after reading this book. You don't have to be a CPA or a tax attorney to understand his presentation.
Frank

Many points of interest and reflections on life events common to us all, regardless of economic status, and how life insurance can be utilized advantageously in them all.
Daniel

As a sequel to the first book, the concepts become clearer and it sheds a whole new light on the finance world!
Alicia

Common sense when you really think about it. Wall Street has us hoodwinked!
Mark

This book is another good read from the same author for me. I find Bryan to be clear and concise in his writing. Enough story to illuminate the subject well but not so much as to bring the reader to YAWN. Bryan writes with authority and with knowledge that a lot of writers do not have.

Thomas

It will expand your knowledge of the art of the possible when it comes to saving money.
Jack

Considering the cultural inertia against it in the mainstream financial world, getting a good and unbiased understanding of permanent life insurance is difficult. Bryan Bloom's book is the clearest and most concise primer on this paradigm-shifting concept that I've read.
SDS

This book teaches you how to capture all the money that slips through our fingers throughout our whole working life and use it to be tax efficient, growth efficient, income and asset protective, and the ability to be your own bank by financing your purchases through yourself so you can build your own wealth instead of building all the Banks' wealth. A MUST, MUST READ!!!
Carl

These are some of the Great Secrets that Wall Street doesn't want the 'average Joe' to know about because it would steer people away from the madness towards a predictable & stress-free financial future.
Jay

Understanding that successful people have always done things differently than most people is a key factor that is explored in the book. Thanks for helping to open minds to think outside the box. It helps people understand that just because

everyone else it still doing the same financial planning; that doesn't make it the best way.
Rich

Dedication

Dedicated to
My Grandchildren:

Emmie Lynn Sederquist
Ellie Leigh Sederquist
Coen Scott Musgrave

Who will receive the legacy of truth discovered today, and represent the next generation charged with carrying the truth forward.

Acknowledgements

Writing a book is a challenging experience and it is not done alone! There are many people who make the words on a page both easily understandable and interesting for the reader.

This book could not have been written without the love and support of family.

First and foremost, I am grateful to my Heavenly Father, the Yahweh of the Old Testament of the Bible, who lets me call him "Abba Father," and His Son, Jesus Christ, who is my personal Lord and Savior.

My earthly family has been indispensable to the of writing this book. I am thankful for the encouragement of my spouse of 36 years; Pam lifts me to heights of excellence and integrity not achievable on my own. I am grateful for her inspiration every day. Our two daughters have participated in bringing my book from concept to reality. Callie Sederquist has been indispensable as a financial professional in her own right. Her knowledge of financial products has expanded my own understanding. Corrie Musgrave did a wonderful job helping me to word sections of the books just right. She served as my consistency editor. She helped me by editing to ensure congruency between the charts and chart discussions. She was also influential in helping me envision Confessions of a CPA as a potential series of books, not just Confessions of a CPA II or III.

My extended family was vital. The way you verbally say something isn't necessarily how you write something. But that is what I did. Jeff and Abby Abbott were my frontline editors. I think it took longer to edit the books than it did to write them. They did an excellent job. They also served the purpose of being you, my target audience. They read the manuscript from your perspective and helped me to bring clarity to portions that were difficult to understand.

I am very fortunate to be associated with other financial professionals that help me hone my skills. I have received valuable support from the professionals at The America Group, in St. Louis, Missouri. Specifically, Bill Maxson and Liz Kelly selfishly help me. I am also privileged to be part of the BreakAway League. An organization founded by Tom Love, an organization that prides itself in "swimming upstream". You will find that this book indeed swims upstream.

Together with Tom, Emily Prendiville, Ken Kendall, John Dwyer, Andy White, Matt Love and Will Slepcevich we have mentored hundreds of financial professionals in the principles you will find within this book.

Lastly, I want to thank you, the reader of Confessions of a CPA. You are not only reading the book, but you are putting it into practice. I have heard story after story of how the principles in these books have helped you. That is the real motivation in my writing. If I can make a difference in another family's life with the lessons I have personally learned, then the effort that goes into writing is worthwhile. Thank you.

Important Disclosures

This book contains a discussion of investments in general and life insurance in detail.

Whether illustrating investment returns or life insurance cash value and death benefits, hypothetical illustrations may not be relied on as a certain prediction of or projection of those results.

Since life insurance is discussed extensively in this book:

Tax-free withdrawals and loans assume that the life insurance policy is properly funded and is not a modified endowment contract. Withdrawals are generally treated first as tax-free recovery of basis and then as taxable income, assuming the policy is not a modified endowment contract.

However, different rules generally apply in the first fifteen policy years, when distributions accompanied by benefit reductions may be taxable prior to basis recovery. Loans from policies that are not classified as modified endowment contracts are generally not subject to tax but may be taxable if the policy lapses, is surrendered, exchanged or otherwise terminated. In the case of a modified endowment contract, loans and withdrawals are taxable to the extent of policy gain and a 10% penalty may apply if taken prior to age 59½. Always confirm the status of a particular loan or withdrawal with a qualified tax advisor. Cash value accumulation may not be guaranteed depending on the type of product selected. Income tax-free death benefits, withdrawals and loans apply to Federal taxes only. State income taxes may apply. Loans and withdrawals will reduce the death benefit. Dividends are declared on an annual basis and may not be consistent from year to year. Dividend projections in this book are based on dividends declared in 2018 and are assumed to remain unchanged during the entire length of the projection.

It is important that you consult with your own qualified tax advisor regarding your particular situation.

Contents

Before You Begin

In the back of this book there are blank pages. Use them to record new thoughts or observations you discover during the reading of this book. When you have an "ah-ha" moment, make sure you write it down.

Forward

I have known Bryan Bloom for more than a decade. At first, I discovered Bryan as an extremely knowledgeable speaker, who was always willing to share his ideas and perspectives with others in the industry. More recently, our relationship has grown into a business partnership, and most importantly into a great friendship. In all the time I have known him, Bryan has demonstrated a willingness to use his forty years as a CPA to "look outside of the box" to find the best solutions for his clients. And when he has discovered better ways to maximize the benefit for his clients, he wants to share his findings so other advisors can help their clients as well.

One of the things that originally attracted me to the financial services business was that there is rarely one right answer to the questions we all face in managing our money. Most of the time, there are many different ways to achieve your financial goals, and if you have a knowledgeable guide, they can help educate you into finding the solution that is most comfortable for you.

Therefore, a key component in choosing your adviser, is to find one who both understands the options available to you and is willing to take time to share the pluses and minuses of several options with you, to help you make decisions that are right for you.

In his book series, *Confessions of a CPA*, Bryan Bloom has taken this one step further. He is not just educating clients, Bryan has taken on the mission of educating the entire financial services industry into rethinking what they have historically been taught and believed. His first book, *Confessions of a CPA: Why What I Was Taught To Be True Turned Out Not To Be*, hits this straight on, and has become a must read book for all financial professionals.

Now in this new book, *Confessions of a CPA: The Capital Equivalent Value of Life Insurance*, Bryan looks at retirement income planning. Most of us spend our entire working careers worrying about accumulation planning, trying to maximize what we are able to set aside and keep, to be able to fund our (ever lengthening) retirement years, when much of the income has stopped. Too often, advisors and clients only look at strategies to accumulate the largest amount of money they can, totally forgetting about the taxes and other costs involved when it becomes time to try to use these dollars. In our country's current financial situation, with spiraling deficits and ever-increasing fixed expenses, the question of just what the taxes will be in the future, when we want to use the dollars, becomes absolutely critical. Many people, and most advisors, are very good on the accumulation phase, but get confused on the proper ways to take the money out. Bryan's approach is to start with the end result, the distribution of these dollars, maximizing the net, after-tax, spendable dollars. Obviously, this "distribution solution" is critical, and makes this book a must read for anyone concerned with their financial future.

I believe it is critical to read this book, and most importantly, find an advisor who is willing to help you implement these strategies of starting or transitioning your existing assets by planning with your ultimate end result in mind.

William N. Maxson, CFP, CLU, ChFC, CFS

What I Believe

In everything we read, we ought to know what the author believes. What drives the author to write what they write? Let me start this book by telling you a little about what I believe financially.

Over the course of our careers, our thoughts and beliefs evolve as we gain experience. As a novice, we begin our careers by applying the theories and principles we learned in school to the real world. We note what works and what doesn't, and we eventually adjust our approach to fit the realities of life.

For myself, finance has been a 40-year career, and I am still learning what works and what does not. But most important has been understanding what drives what I do, and what motivates me to keep going.

I have discovered that *what* I do is less important than *why* I do it. "*What*" describes a job, but "*why*" describes motivation, conviction and urgency, and it is the "*why*" that encapsulates a series of my beliefs that catapult me toward a real mission in life:

- I believe that what we are taught to be true ought to be true.
- I believe that we should challenge and test what is taught until we know that it is true.
- I believe that we should pay taxes once — and only once — on the money we earn.

When we trade our time for someone else's dollars, that money is fair game for The Administration to tax. That is "earned income."

- I do not believe that what our money earns should be taxed — ever! "Unearned income" should be off the radar screen of the IRS.

- I believe that what we receive from Social Security should not be taxed for two reasons: one, it is unearned income, and two, it has already been taxed once when it was "earned income."

- I believe that wealth distribution is more important than wealth accumulation. Therefore, I believe that we should challenge the financial planning status quo and stop following each other off the financial cliff.

- I believe that people today are unknowingly and unnecessarily transferring hundreds of thousands of dollars of their wealth to financial institutions and to the government.

- I believe those transfers can be recaptured, recouped and strategically redeployed to shift the possibility of financial success back to us.

As these beliefs have developed and become foundational to my career, I have never had as much fun as I have today helping people uncover these truths for themselves.

That is why I have written this series of books, *Confessions of a CPA*, which expose some of the lessons I've learned the hard way in my career as I have sought to apply what I was taught:

- In book one, *Confessions of a CPA: Why What I Was Taught To Be True Has Turned Out Not To Be*, I challenged some of the traditional approaches to implementing a financial plan and provided alternatives that lead to financial freedom.

- In book two, *Confessions of a CPA: The Truth About Life Insurance*, I examined strategic approaches to life insurance that leverage and unlock the economic value of life insurance during your lifetime, therefore increasing the value from your other retirement assets.

- In this third book, *Confessions of a CPA: The Capital Equivalent Value of Life Insurance*, I take it all one step further and answer questions like:
  - What if permanent life insurance was your only retirement asset?
  - What would other assets have to be worth to provide the same retirement cash flows as your permanent life insurance policy (the Capital Equivalent Value)?
  - How can you calculate the Capital Equivalent Value of your permanent life insurance policy?

Before we consider the living benefits of life insurance and its economic value in this book, we cannot ignore the traditional value of life insurance and what it can provide when life ends prematurely, and all the hopes and dreams of your family vanish.

My good friend John Butler told his story at a convention of financial professionals:

"My story goes back over forty years, but who could see into the future forty years? When my father retired from the Air Force in 1960, he was forty-seven years old and had to keep working as my sister and I were still in high school. He was a man who had graduated from the school of hard knocks in rural Illinois. He was orphaned early, went to Chaddock School for Boys in Quincy, IL, and on to the US Army at the age of eighteen. Since he had lived through the Great Depression as a young man, he had learned that cash was what a person needed to make their way through life. He was always a saver and kept very close track of his money.

I remember one incident when I found a $20 bill in our driveway and it took him three days to figure out where he had spent the $20 bill that was missing from his wallet. I did get to keep the money after waiting out his memory, but my dad always had money for the things I needed, — new shoes, clothes that fit, and for other unexpected demands for money that we all contend with as we operate our households. When I was still in junior high school, he taught me how to reconcile the family checkbook. I had no conception of what all the numbers meant.

Nevertheless, we struggled through the checkbook reconciliation process.

All of that leads us back to the retirement day from the Air Force. We moved to Ft. Worth, Texas, and my dad set out to sell life insurance for a major life insurance company. His training through the life insurance company was on how to sell life insurance the life insurance company way. It is a tough business, and without today's tools and concepts, it was a *very* tough business. His journey was brief, but he did believe in the product that he was selling.

He believed in whole life insurance. He had caught on to the theory of using life insurance to both save money and prepare for the unexpected events of life. For some reason, he purchased a whole life policy on my younger sister. The policy was for a face value of $10,000 with a premium of less than $100 per year. That was big money 45 years ago. He was getting her off to a good start by saving money in a whole life policy.

We have learned that life consists of both expected and unexpected events. The unexpected happened on October 8, 1971, just north of Tonica, Illinois, when my sister's car was hit by an oncoming car that had spun out of control. She was killed instantly, probably never even knowing what hit her. She was 21 years old, a senior in the nursing program at the University of Iowa. You know, when you leave this earth you have no idea of what is coming for the people you leave behind. But, you should know what to expect for yourself. My sister knew Jesus and she left plenty of evidence.

Of course, the life insurance policy paid the death benefit to my father. With the money suddenly becoming liquid, he invested in my start-up grain elevator business in Illinois. That money grew and grew, providing a living for me to raise my family and giving my father a great deal of satisfaction seeing that money at work. *It is impossible to know exactly how much money that $10,000 has made, but it started a family business that ran grain* *elevators for 20 years. The money was then moved into farmland where it has continued to provide income for my family. Today the rate of return on the value of the farm exceeds the ability of any financial calculator. You could say that the rate of return on that $10,000 is almost infinite."*

That is just one story of what a life insurance policy has accomplished over more than 40 years. Who knows what the policies purchased today will do for the owners in the future? How will the money be used — for enjoyment, for starting a business, to save a business in a cash crunch, for a college education, or for retirement? In every case, it will make life better no matter what happens.

Capital Equivalent Value Defined

Financial assets can be very difficult to value. When we consider what something is worth, we often think of what its rate of return is. However, that can be very short-sided for a number of reasons.

First, when it comes to finding value in something, it is only worth what it can be traded for. Long ago, our economy was based on directly trading "goods for goods" or "talents for goods." Today we have an intermediary: "money." Now, we take our "time and talents" to someone who needs what we have to offer in order to generate a product or service that others value. Without our time and talents, they have nothing. As the process works backward, money is exchanged for that final product or service, some of which is kept by our employer and some is given to us in exchange for our time and talents. So, what is our time and talent really worth? We may think of it as the money we received, but it is so much more. What benefit did those dollars get for you when you exchanged them for something you wanted or needed? This is the true value of the asset called your time and talent. Money is merely an intermediary; it's just money. The true value is based on benefits.

Second, benefits can only be claimed as they are expressed in dollars. In other words, you can only spend dollars — you can't spend a rate of return. All of our fascination with rates of return is merely a distraction from what is really important: what benefit can be derived?

A couple of simple questions frame it up for me:

1. When I come to the end of my life, which will have been more important — the rate of return, or the money I had available to spend?

2. If given the choice, which would you choose?

    A. A $5,000,000 nest egg that would provide you with $200,000 per year to live on in retirement, or

    B. A $3,000,000 nest egg that would provide you with $180,000 per year tax-exempt to live on in retirement?

Those in pursuit of maximum accumulation of funds are going to be focused on rate of return and would likely prefer the $5,000,000 nest egg. This is likely the situation because they are focused only on accumulation of money and not on the distribution of wealth.

Permanent life insurance happens to be one of the most difficult assets to value because its benefits are more complex and cannot be easily shown as a straightforward sum of money like other assets. So how do we put a true value on life insurance? Do we merely concentrate on the accumulation of its cash values? Do we emphasize the value of the death benefits, as in John's story? Or is there a way to value both at the same time, as it relates to you as the owner of the asset?

The Capital Equivalent Value of Life Insurance provides the answer. Capital Equivalent Value is defined as the sum of money a financial asset would have to grow to in order to provide the same benefit of another financial asset (like a permanent life insurance policy). Therefore, Capital Equivalent Value is a benefit-based calculation. In the case of a difficult-to-value asset like permanent life insurance, Capital Equivalent Value shows what any other asset would need to accumulate to in order to provide the same benefits that the life insurance policy provides.

Mount Everest

Mount Everest has the distinction of being the tallest mountain in the world. It stands at 29,035 feet. Its top is the most desirous summit of all mountain climbers. Story after story, documentary after documentary, the quest for the top is filmed and chronicled. But is the summit really the goal?

A few startling statistics:

From 1924 through August 2015, there have been 4,093 individual people who have stood on the summit of Mt. Everest. Some have paid as much as $85,000 in their final quest of the top. A total of 282 individuals have died in their pursuit. The death-to-summit ratio is almost 7% (this is an important number to remember as you read ahead). Out of every 100 people that make it to the top, seven die.

More startling is the statistic that 56% of all the deaths that occurred on Mount Everest occurred after they had made it to the summit. That is right. There are 157 people who are counted in both statistics: those that succeeded (made it to the summit) and those that failed (died on the mountain). So, did they succeed or fail? (source: alanarnette.com Everest 2016)

Much is the same when it comes to financial planning. What is your goal? Is it to accumulate the biggest number? Or, is your goal to get down the mountain safely? Which would you rather have: $5,000,000 and reaching the top, knowing that if you withdrew more than 4% of the nest egg ($200,000) you had an unacceptable probability of running out of money? Or getting 60 percent of the way to the top ($3,000,000), but knowing that your probability of running out of money was low, even when withdrawing perhaps even more, after tax ($180,000)?

It has everything to do with what you are concentrating on: the bigger number (the better rate of return), or the benefits that can be achieved if you set your sights on your distributions.

On the way up the retirement mountain are you minimizing your taxes as much as possible so you can accumulate more? Or are you paying your fair share as you climb, so when you descend you don't have a tax burden hanging around your neck? Do you believe as I do, that we should only be required to pay taxes once, only on the money we earn and not on the money that our money earns? It makes a significant difference in your retirement years.

Compound Interest

The more I study how wealth works, the more I'm convinced that Albert Einstein was right when he said, "Compound interest is the 8th wonder of the world. He who understands it, earns it." He was really onto something here. However, he would have been more accurate had he added, "as long as he doesn't spend it." Perhaps he should have said, *uninterrupted* compound interest is the 8th wonder of the world — he who understands it, *earns it and keeps it*.

I was always taught to understand and respect the exponential curve that reveals this miracle. Indeed, a dollar earning a dime is not just $1.10. It is the continual earning power of not just the dollar but also all of the dimes in the earning cycle over and over again. There is more power in the dimes accumulating and earning than in the original dollar earning. The cycle continues as long as it is not interrupted. This is the key to financial freedom: just don't spend your money, ever.

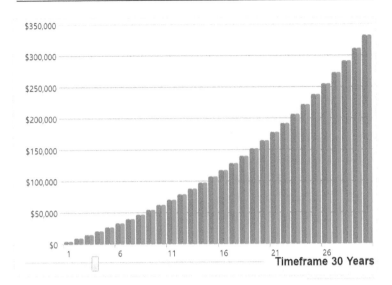

The "Miracle of Compound Interest"
Green: uninterrupted compound interest.
Red: interest allowed to compound uninterrupted.

Well, that is just downright silly! We save money in order to spend money. But if you do, the miracle disappears.

If you save $5,000 per year for 30 years earning 5%, and don't spend it, you would have over $300,000.

However, if your spent your savings every five years, in 30 years you would have slightly more than $25,000. Is the miracle gone? No, it has merely been transferred to someone else.

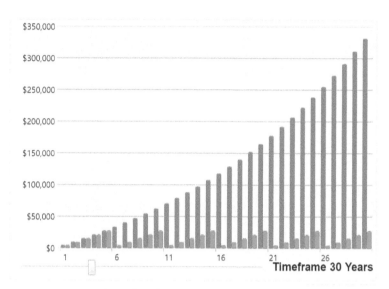

Resetting the account every 5 years
Green: uninterrupted compound interest.
Red: compound interest interrupted every 5 years.

By not understanding this concept, we unknowingly and unnecessarily transfer the miracle to:

- Universities: when you pay tuition from your compounding account.
- The IRS: when you pay your income taxes from your compounding account.
- Financial Institutions: when you pay your account fees from your compounding account.
- The Car Dealership: when you pay for your car from your compounding account.

- Your local grocer: when you pay for your groceries from your compounding account.

What? My groceries? Yes, a very subtle financial principle that many of us never realize is that everything we purchase, we finance. Everything! Even when we pay cash. When you borrow money from the bank to purchase your car, you are borrowing from the bank and paying interest "now." But, when you pay cash for your car — or even your groceries — you are borrowing from your future by interrupting the compounding interest. You are just going to have that much less during your retirement. More on this important concept later.

Let's get real: you must spend money. Perhaps the best advice to give is that when you spend money on something you can afford from your paycheck, pay cash. But when you want to spend money on something that won't be covered by your paycheck, borrow the funds. Plan on paying it back from within your budget, from future paychecks. Never spend your savings or investments, interrupting the compounding.

This first became evident to me a few years after I had begun to develop a compounding investment strategy of my own. There was a year, early on, in which the taxes due on the growth of my investment account exceeded my ability to pay the taxes out of pocket. I had the money to pay the taxes, but it was contained in the investments. In order to pay my taxes that year I needed to withdraw the money out of the investments to send to the IRS. There are two problems here.

First, the taxes we pay are either a direct reduction of our current lifestyle (paying the taxes out of pocket) or a direct reduction of our future lifestyle. Let's say the tax was $1,000. The choice to pay it out of pocket is to reduce my checking account balance by $1,000. This means I can't spend that money on anything else today and it will never earn another dime for me again — a current and future lifestyle reduction. If I didn't have enough money in the checkbook, I would need to redeem some of my investments to pay the tax — investments that represented money I was planning to spend on my future lifestyle. Either way, the IRS intrudes on my life when they tax the money my money earns.

Second, when I reduce my future lifestyle, the reduction is compounded. It is compounded because, in this example, not only will my withdrawn investment never earn a dime again, but it has lost its potential to compound.

In this example, what did a $1,000 tax cost my future lifestyle? It cost the $1,000 tax payment and all the interest that the $1,000 plus its earnings would have earned. If this tax were due when I was 40 years of age and I could have earned 5% on my investment account, the $1,000 withdrawal cost my future lifestyle $3,386 (at the retirement age of 65).

As soon as you withdraw money from a compounding account, the compounding is reset. The new compound interest curve is flatter and longer.

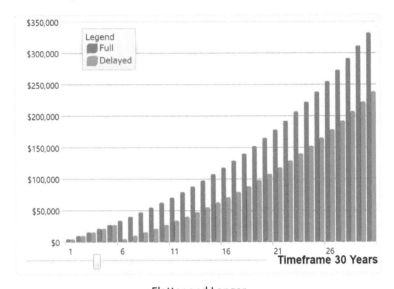

Flatter and Longer
Green: uninterrupted compound interest
Red: compounding interrupted just once
(notice how the gap gets larger as time elapses)

The second time I noticed this happening was when my daughters wanted to go to college. I was always taught to save and invest for college because you will never be able to pay for it out of your budget (your current lifestyle). So I did. The result was a retirement compound interest curve that was flatter and longer.

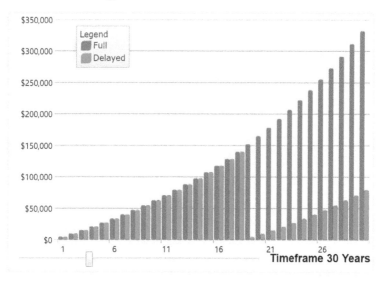

Paying for College
Green: uninterrupted compound interest.
Red: interrupted compound interest to pay tuition.
Who gets the miracle? The college!

If I add up the cost of the tax and tuitions paid in this simple example, they do not account for the reduction of my compound interest curve from where I should have been and where I actually was. The difference between what I spent and what I was supposed to have were light years apart. You can see the effect of interrupting the compound interest curve:

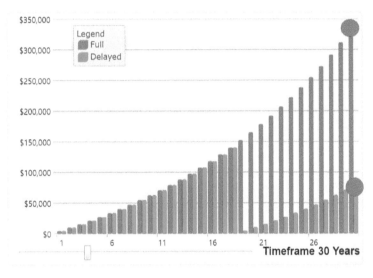

The only exponential experience is what you DON'T have!
Green: uninterrupted compound interest.
Red: compounding interrupted.

The logical conclusion is that Einstein was wrong. Compound interest is not the 8th wonder of the world! But, Einstein can't be wrong!

Everything We Purchase We Finance

Many fathers launch their children into adulthood with two lessons:

1. Never enter into debt, because then you will pay interest.

2. Never pay more for something than it is worth, which of course you will if you have to pay interest.

Two ways of saying the same thing — but that was dad!

I was always taught to save before I spent anything. Always save, then spend. Never the other way around. So that is what I did. I'd save for a car, then I'd buy the car. The cost of this approach to me was the delayed satisfaction of owning my first car. A small price to pay to implement such a sound financial strategy, right?

Meanwhile, my friends, who couldn't stave off the purchase of their first car, borrowed money and paid it back. Just as the first car was paid off, they started the cycle all over again.

Who was better off?

According to dad, I was better off because I never paid interest. In reality, my friends and I were both at the same point at the end of every purchase cycle: zero.

I would save, then spend my savings back to zero, while my friends borrowed and worked their way back up to zero by paying off their debts. We were in the same position — zero! What happened?

The lesson to be learned is that there really is no difference between saving and spending or borrowing and paying back. The lending position is easy to understand; you pay interest. The saving position is a bit more subtle; when you spend what you save, you don't earn interest.

Either way, paying interest or not receiving interest is a cost of the purchase. Everything we purchase, we finance — we just don't realize it. And it doesn't matter whether it is a loan from the bank to purchase a car, or a loan from our future lifestyle to purchase a bag of groceries; both have a cost beyond the cost of the car or the groceries themselves.

The only difference is when the cost is felt. In the case of bank financing, the cost is felt while you are making the payments. In the case of paying cash, the cost isn't felt until 40 years later when you have less to spend during your retirement years.

I understand that this may all seem small and inconsequential, but over the years, understanding how to purchase common goods now can add up to a significantly higher quality of life for you in retirement.

Despite what many of us learned, it is only when combining the saving and borrowing financial strategies that true economic value emerges.

Saving AND Borrowing

The miracle of compound interest is unachievable whenever you spend what you have saved and invested. But, if everything we purchase has an ultimate cost over and above the sticker price, (because everything we purchase we finance), is there a better way?

Yes.

We need to learn how to combine saving AND borrowing at the same time. And how can we do this? Leave what you have saved and invested to compound uninterrupted, and spend someone else's money when you want to purchase something.

This will always work when the cost of borrowing is less than the gain on your savings and investments. That is the concept of arbitrage:

"Arbitrage is the simultaneous purchase and sale of an asset (cash) to profit from a difference in the price (interest rates). It is a trade that profits by exploiting the price differences of identical or similar financial instruments (cash) on different markets (savings market and debt market) or in different forms." (Source: Investopedia.com). My interpretation in parenthesis.

What if interest rates are inverted? What if the interest rate cost of borrowing is more than the rate of return of your savings or investments?

Over a short period of time, it depends on the sheer volume of actual dollars. The larger your savings and investments balance and the smaller the amount of your loan outstanding, you may still gain a larger number of dollars in your savings and investments than dollars you will have to pay to borrow money.

Here is an example. Let's suppose you are 50 years old with a $200,000 investment balance and want to purchase a $50,000 car.

Since you have the money, you may likely choose to pay cash, because you don't want to have to pay interest or pay more for something than it is worth. Let's examine this decision.

When you remove the $50,000 from your investment account, will you permanently remove that money? Over time, some will likely return the $50,000 removed from the account, but few will restore the gain that money missed earning because it was out of the account, and none will restore what the gain would have gained had it never been removed from the account in the first place (the value of the compounding). Here is what it actually cost you to purchase the $50,000 vehicle from your savings or investment account. I am assuming you are earning 5% in this savings or investment account:

Over the **first year**, that vehicle actually cost you:

- $50,000 purchase price *plus*
- $2,500 gains you did not earn in your investment account *equals*
- $52,500 actual cost of the car

Over the **first five years**, that vehicle actually cost you:

- $50,000 purchase price *plus*
- $13,814.08 gains you did not earn in your investment account *equals*
- $63,814.08 actual cost of the car

Why is this such an odd amount? Because it reflects not only the gain on the $50,000 investment that is no longer in the account, but also the gain on the gains that are no longer in the account.

What is the **cost to your retirement**? If you retire at age 65 the vehicle cost you:

- $50,000 car purchase price *plus*
- $53,946.41 gains you did not earn in your investment account *equals*
- $103,946.41 actual cost to your retirement nest egg, funds not available to your retirement lifestyle

What is the cost of this vehicle **to your heirs**? If you live to your life expectancy of 85:

- $50,000 car purchase price *plus*
- $225,800.77 gains you did not earn in your investment account *equals*
- $275,800.77 actual cost of the car to your heirs, funds they will never inherit

That is just one vehicle! What if you purchased a new car every five years? The cost of driving to work where you may be building your retirement nest egg through your 401(k) is easily over $1,000,000.

Now, what if you could purchase the vehicles without interrupting the compounding of your savings or investment account?

By combining the concept of saving and borrowing together, you begin to piece together the answer.

Most financial institutions will accept your compounding account balance as collateral to borrow their money. Your money continues to grow, you just can't spend it while it is being held as collateral. With near perfect collateral such as your actual account, banks will likely extend to you their money at their best rates.

Does this sound like the way you purchased your home? It should, because this is exactly the way we obtain a mortgage to purchase a house. The personal asset used as collateral is your house. People do this every day. Why don't we do this with everything else? We don't because we think we can "afford" to pay cash, so that must be best. So, rather than pledge that cash as collateral, we give it up. As described above, that is an "unaffordable" transaction, but we do it every day.

In my book, *Confessions of a CPA — The Truth About Life Insurance*, I describe the pros and cons of many of the accounts that a financial institution will accept as collateral. That book shows that a permanent life insurance contract is the perfect financial instrument to pledge as collateral back to the life insurance company in order to borrow their money.

Here is how it works:

1. Look at your permanent life insurance contract as a financial institution unto itself.

The first step is to purchase a contract and fund it. Much like a new bank needing to capitalize itself (establish a serious balance of funds from which to lend), you need to purchase a permanent life insurance contract that you fund to a serious balance of funds against which to borrow.

2. When dividends are paid, the life insurance company will provide you several options regarding how to apply or accept those dividends. Choose to have your dividends purchase "paid up additions." This choice allows both your cash values to compound and your death benefits to grow.

Now that you have built up sufficient cash values to pledge as collateral to borrow funds from the life insurance company, you can:

3. Begin to use your new leverage to fund your major purchases. Most of the time, you can request a loan from the life insurance company with a single sheet of paper or phone call. No applications, no credit checks, no financial disclosures, and no waiting time. Funds are transferred to your checking account the day after you make the request.

Because these funds represent a loan from the life insurance company, they are not taxable income to you, this is much like your mortgage loan which was not taxable income to you when you purchased your home with borrowed funds.

4. Other than the interest rate, the terms of the loan are up to you. As long as you have

enough collateral, you can pay back your loan whenever your want — or never at all.

5. If you die with a loan outstanding, the principle of the loan outstanding and any interest that wasn't paid will be recovered from your death benefit that would otherwise be paid to your heirs. Literally, your dead self is repaying the loan.

What about retirement?

In retirement you can choose to never repay the outstanding loan. Your eventual death benefit will cover what you borrowed to finance your retirement.

Let's look at an example. Assume you are a 55-year-old couple who can afford to pay $100,000 each per year for ten years toward your retirement, either from your cash flows or by redirecting other investment balances. That represents a total commitment of $1,000,000 toward your retirement.

If you are wondering where you can find $100,000 per year, remember that the kids may be out of college. You are no longer paying tuition, room, board, and expenses; those can be redirected. If they have sucked you dry of all your retirement dollars, you have to start saving in a big way at this point anyway, or you won't retire when you want. After all, in the years prior to college you wondered how you would pay for college, but you did anyway.

If your funding ability is not $100,000 per year, or you would like more cash flow in retirement, all of the numbers in this example are scalable up or down.

If you are younger, you have the ability to start earlier, which means you will be able to pay at a lower annual commitment rate in order to accomplish what this 55-year-old couple will accomplish.

Now, immediately upon signing their permanent life insurance contracts, this couple will each begin with approximately $850,000 to $950,000 of death benefits, depending on their health and whether they are male or female. When they retire ten years later, they will have accumulated approximately $1,082,000 of cash values. That should not seem like a lot, after all, your total deposits were $1,000,000. However, remember the Mount Everest story — would you rather have a bigger nest egg or more retirement cash flow? Keep reading.

As the couple begins their retirement years at age 66 (to coincide with approximately the beginning of their social security payouts), they can begin to take loans from the insurance company that will be recovered from their ultimate death benefits at the rate of approximately $70,000 per year.

One of the requirements of the tax laws that define life insurance (Technical And Miscellaneous Revenue Act of 1988 (TAMRA) and The Deficit Reduction Act of 1984 (DEFRA)) is that the death benefits of a life insurance contract must increase in value or you have to take the annual dividends as taxable income. To avoid this taxable event, our choice was to reinvest the dividends as "paid up additions," thereby increasing both the cash values as well as the death benefits.

Because this couple chose this method of receiving dividends, their combined death benefits have grown from $1,800,000 in the first year to now more than $2,010,000 ten years later.

As they take loans to finance their retirement, the chart below represents their combined life insurance contract values.

Year	Cash Outflow (loan)	Cumulative Cash Outflow	Remaining Collateral	Death Benefit
10	0	0	1.100,000	2,010,000
11	70,000	70,000	1,075,000[1]	1,973,000[2]
12	70,000	140,000	1,031,000	1,933,000
13	70,000	210,000	1,004,000	1,892,000
14	70,000	280,000	977,000	1,849,000
15	70,000	350,000	948,000	1,804,000
20	70,000	700,000	784,000	1,550,000
25	70,000	1,050,000	585,000	1,250,000
30[3]	70,000	1,400,000	338,000	905,000
31	70,000	1,470,000	283,000	831,000[4]

[1] Why does the remaining collateral go down less than the amount of the first loan? For two reasons. First, this life insurance contract is coming from a company who utilizes the "non-direct recognition" method of granting dividends. That dividend-granting method ignores loans outstanding when they grant the dividend. The dividend is granted on the gross cash values, not the remaining collateral. In this example, the gross cash value in year 11 is $1,130,000. This represents the value of not interrupting the compounding of any financial asset. Second, the remaining collateral represents the prior year's cash value plus dividends granted minus loans outstanding. Consequently, the remaining collateral goes down slower in the early years than the loan itself. (For a fuller explanation of "non-direct recognition," please refer to *Confessions of a CPA — The Truth About Life Insurance*)

[2] Why does the death benefit go down less than the amount of the first loan? The answer is basically for the same reasons

that the remaining collateral goes down slower. Cash value plus dividends granted minus loans outstanding.

[3] Year 30 (age 85) represents the life expectancy of a healthy 55 year old. At this point in the chart, notice that there has been a cumulative $1,400,000 distributed to this couple, and the remaining death benefit is just below what their total deposit was. If death occurs at normal life expectancy, the cash outflow between this couple and their heirs would be $1,300,000 more than they put in ($1,400,000 cash outflow during lifetime plus $905,000 cash outflow at death minus $1,000,000 total invested).

However, it is unlikely that both partners of this couple will die at exactly the same time. Consequently, one of the two will receive approximately $450,000 to supplement the rest of their survivorship lifestyle.

[4] Why do the death benefits begin to go down faster than the amount of the new loan in year 31? Because, at this point, the loan outstanding is not only the principle borrowed each year, but also the interest due each year that hasn't been paid. The dividends in year 31 are no longer enough to cover the interest on the loan outstanding in year 31.

You must make sure that there is always enough collateral to cover the loan outstanding. Remember, it is the collateral that gives you the permission to borrow from the life insurance company. If you violate the terms of the collateral requirement, the life insurance company will give you two choices:

1. Begin shoring up your collateral by paying the interest due on the cumulative loans outstanding each year.

2. Cancel the life insurance contract and the loan outstanding and keep the cash value that represents the remaining collateral after the repayment of the loan.

Neither solution is advantageous to you.

Because you no longer have any collateral capacity for additional loans, you will cease to receive the annual loan distributions and you will need to start paying the interest.

If you cancel the life insurance contract, all of the previous loans — up to what you have paid in the form of premiums — remain tax-exempt. They represent a return of your principle. But the excess over your cumulative premiums is no longer considered loan proceeds. They are recategorized by the Internal Revenue Service as "deemed distributions" and reportable as taxable income in the year you cancel the life insurance contract.

The life insurance company doesn't care which you choose; they are in the perfect position. The loan they have extended to you is likely at market interest rates and represents an adequate financial investment, or they can redeem the cash value used as collateral and reinvest it at market interest rates.

A well-designed life insurance contract will include annual loan distributions that extend for five years past your life expectancy and will provide for a death benefit to at least age 100. Your specific family history may dictate longer periods. It is extremely important to work with a life insurance professional who understands these concepts and will work with you to monitor the contract's performance on an annual basis. You may need to make adjustments along the way.

Why Life Insurance Works

Life insurance is the best asset to use in this strategy because of what the Internal Revenue Code provides in regard to its taxation.

The Deficit Reduction Act of 1984 (DEFRA) and The Technical and Miscellaneous Revenue Act of 1988 (TAMRA), together gave a new definition to what would be considered a life insurance contract and what would be considered an annuity. The tax laws give preferential tax treatment to life insurance over annuities. The limits of DEFRA and TAMRA must be adhered to or what you thought would be tax-exempt (life insurance) will be merely tax-deferred (annuities).

The pertinent life insurance provisions in the Internal Revenue Code are:

26 U.S. Code § 7702: This section defines what qualifies as a life insurance contract and what does not. This is important because only life insurance contracts receive the most favorable tax treatment.

26 U.S. Code § 101 (a): This section defines certain death benefits paid at death that are exempt from income taxation.

26 U.S. Code § 101(g)(1): This section specifically exempts from income taxation certain accelerated death benefits paid during a person's life.

26 U.S. Code § 72(e): This section differentiates between an annuity (taxable income) and a life insurance contract (tax-exempt income), specifically:

- Any loan distributions for which a portion of the value of the contract is assigned is not received as an annuity (and consequently, tax-exempt).

- Any dividend earned is not included in gross income to the extent the dividend is retained by the insurer as a premium (for the purpose of purchasing "paid up additions" with the dividends).

26 U.S. Code § 72(e)(5): This section excludes all life insurance contracts issued prior to August 13, 1982 from the provisions of Code section 72(e). This is what is commonly known as the grandfather clause, not subjecting prior life insurance contracts to the constraints put on new life insurance contracts.

26 U. S. Code § 86: This section provides for the second taxation of social security and Tier 1 railroad retirement benefits because of other taxable income.

As a requirement of TAMRA, the United States Government Accounting Office (GAO) was to report to Congress regarding the effectiveness of the revised tax treatment of life insurance and the policy justification for, and the practical implications of, the present treatment of earnings on the cash surrender value of life insurance and annuity contracts in light of the Tax Reform Act of 1986.

In their report they made the following observations:

"The basic purpose of life insurance is to provide protection against income loss to beneficiaries who are often dependents of the insured. The death of the insured terminates the whole life insurance policy. The accumulated interest income or inside buildup in a life insurance policy is not taxed when paid to the beneficiary on the death of the insured. Death benefits have been exempt from federal income tax on welfare and humanitarian grounds because they are usually paid to a family that has suffered the loss of the primary earner." (Page 25 of the report)

"If a policyholder borrows the inside buildup from his or her life insurance policy, the amount borrowed is considered a transfer of capital, not a realization of income, and, therefore, is not subject to taxation. This reasoning is in accord with tax policy on other types of loans, such as consumer loans or home mortgages. These loans are merely transfers of capital or savings from one person to another through a financial intermediary. The ability to borrow against a life insurance policy means that the interest income that is supposed to be building up to fund death benefits can instead be a source of untaxed current income. If the loans are not repaid, the inside buildup will never be taxed; death benefits will simply be reduced by the amount of the loan. Thus, policyholders have the use of tax-free income for purposes other than insurance at the expense of reduced death benefits for their beneficiaries." (Page 27 of the report) Source: TAX POLICY: Tax Treatment of Life Insurance and Annuity Accrued Interest. January 1990. United States General Accounting Office

Report to the Chairman, Committee on Finance, U.S. Senate, and the Chairman, Committee on Ways and Means, House of Representatives.

You may be thinking that a life insurance strategy has passed you by because of your age. You may be thinking that now that the children are grown and on their own, you don't need life insurance. You may not need life insurance, but you should want what the life insurance tax code does for you.

How Life Insurance Works

In a traditional sense, life insurance isn't really life insurance — it is death insurance. It isn't really for you to benefit from, but it is for those you care about to benefit from. Life insurance provides cash at just the time when cash is needed most: when the unexpected happens too soon.

However, most life insurance policies never pay this ultimate death benefit.

Sometimes it is designed in such a way that it will probably never pay the death benefit. The premium is structured in such a way that you either plan to, or are forced to, discontinue a life insurance contract after a certain period of time. Either the premium is no longer affordable, or you have reached an age and a stage in life that you don't need the coverage any longer.

Other times, the life insurance contract is provided to a certain group of individuals. If you are no longer a member of the group, you are no longer eligible to keep paying the premiums and the policy is terminated. This often happens when we terminate our employment. What if your next employer doesn't offer a group life insurance contract? What if this is your final employer prior to your retirement? Most group life insurance contracts are not portable. You can't take the contract with you, and if your health has deteriorated by the time you are no longer eligible for a group plan, you may not be eligible to purchase an individual plan.

Less than 2% of all life insurance contracts ever pay a death benefit.

The greatest financial transfer during your lifetime could very well be your life insurance policy. So, be careful to implement a strategy that uses life insurance carefully. Find a financial professional who is skilled at using a life insurance policy as described and ask for assistance. When a life insurance policy does not pay a death benefit, the premiums paid are not returned to you. In addition, what you could have otherwise earned on that money is also lost forever.

When you terminate your life insurance, does the life insurance company return your premiums because you did not die? No! How long do they keep your premiums? Forever!

Financial institutions understand the secret of the miracle of compound interest: minimize the number of interruptions to the compounding of the money. When you don't die on time, you transfer the miracle of all that money to them.

How could life insurance be the greatest financial transfer of your life? Think about it. You are 25 years old. You and your spouse decide that to support the family you plan on having you need $1,000,000 of death benefits between now and when you retire. By then, your assets can provide what your survivors need.

But money is tight, so you opt for the least expensive option: a series of 10-year term life insurance policies that you choose to renew every 10 years when the premium is scheduled to go up.

At age 25, you are at the zenith of health and can obtain a 10-year level premium term life insurance policy (with a waiver of premium in the case of disability) for $27.25 per month for 10 years.

- Total expenditure: $27.25 x 120 months = $3,270.

- Actual cost: $4,249 (because you could have accumulated this amount at interest if you did not give it to the insurance company, you not only spent the $3,270 but also transferred what it could have earned and what the interest you did not earn could have earned (assuming an interest rate of 5%))

- Lifetime cost: $48,725 (because the life insurance did not return any of these premiums or the interest they earned on your money, you have lost that money for a lifetime)

That is just the first 10-year policy! What if you continue this strategy and purchase a new 10-year policy, every 10 years, to replace the previous one?

The lifetime expenditure for your policy between the ages of:

- 35-45: $42,254 (second 10-year policy)
- 45-55: $73,162 (third 10-year policy)
- 55-65: $144,759 (fourth 10-year policy)

Your plan worked! You have made it to retirement, you have accumulated enough assets to financially replace yourself and you no longer need any death insurance. Your total lifetime expenditure is $308,900.

This could be the largest single financial transfer you will likely ever make in your lifetime!

Now, please do not read this and think that you should not purchase term life insurance. You should have a level of life insurance death benefits that equals your human life value. You are the financial engine that runs your family. How would your family's financial future be financed if you were no longer around? Whatever amount of money that would take is your human life value. You must have an amount equal to this until your assets can replace your human life value. Most people can only afford the term life insurance costs, and must opt for this method. Fewer can afford the larger financial outlays that are required for a permanent life insurance policy.

It is precisely these vast sums of money that make a life insurance company tick. Without having to pay death benefits for 98% of the policies, life insurance companies are profitable.

But, what about the 2% that do wind up transferring millions of dollars out of the hands of the insurance companies into the hands of beneficiaries of individuals who die prematurely? The whole premise falls apart if there are too many premature deaths that pay these death benefits.

That is why the Federal Government requires that life insurance companies set aside a certain amount of money (called reserves), in case there aren't enough people paying $27.25 per month to cover a $1,000,000 claim.

Where do the reserves come from? Over time, they can come from enough $27.25 per month premium payers, but what if there are not enough? Enter the equity partners of the life insurance company — that is you and me when we purchase overfunded permanent life insurance policies.

That same 25-year-old who purchased a series of 10-year term policies could have purchased an overfunded permanent life insurance policy for a monthly premium of $1,769 per month for the next 480 months. That would be a total expenditure of over $849,000 for a permanent death benefit that would provide $1,000,000 or more to his beneficiaries at his death. He doesn't need to die on time. The policy is designed to pay a death benefit whenever he dies — not according to some predetermined scheduled.

A quick look would indicate that he is going to trade $1,769 for $1,000,000 of death benefits available from day one of his policy. Over the 480-month period of time, he will pay the $849,000 in monthly installments of $1,769 per month. Now, trading $849,000 over this period of time for $1,000,000 doesn't seem like a good deal on the surface, but it is far better than having no death benefit at all if he doesn't die by age 65. That's zero benefit for a lifetime cost of $308,900.

Now, you might say, "Why would he ever do this when there are better ways to invest your money!"

He would do this because the benefit is not $1,000,000 for an investment of $849,000; it is actually far greater, as I will discuss later.

And you might ask, "Why would the insurance company ever do this if the return is 'far greater' for the policy owner?"

The reason is because the insurance company needs equity partners to accumulate enough reserves to sell their term life insurance policies. These term policies represent their overall profit because the company pays out the death benefit on them only 2% of the time but keeps the premiums forever, and to reward the policyholder of overpaid permanent life insurance (for essentially providing them with the equity they need for their business model to work), the life insurance company returns a portion of their profits to the policyholders in the form of a dividend.

So, the company and the policyholder both receive a return on their investment — both parties win. Additionally, the policyholder happens to receive a far greater benefit than the dividend, and that is what I am building up to in this book.

Enter the Internal Revenue Code (IRC).

According to the provisions of TAMRA and DEFRA, the IRC mandates that either the dividends of a life insurance policy must be paid out to the owners taxable, or if kept in the policy cash values to compound tax deferred, the death benefits have to go up each and every year. By the 40th year in our example of the 25 year old, his death benefit would have grown from $1,000,000 to almost $4,200,000.

According to the IRC, your death benefits are exempt from income taxes, your dividends accumulate tax deferred, and you can extract wealth from your life insurance contract as loans against the ultimate death benefits. The proceeds from a loan of any type are tax exempt. Think back to when you purchased your car and financed $20,000 of the purchase from your local bank. Did you have to report $20,000 as taxable income on your income tax return? No, loan proceeds are tax exempt.

This isn't rocket science. It really is that simple. You just need a life insurance professional that understands how to construct and administer such a life insurance contract. Mountain climbing guides are skilled at not only getting you up the mountain, they are skilled at getting you off the mountain as well. Certain life insurance professionals have these same skills as you face the financial mountain. If you wonder if your financial advisor or life insurance professional have these skills, just ask them for the "exit strategy" they have planned for you. Likely, their plan is only to get you up the mountain, not off the mountain. Who has your exit strategy in mind? Just ask. You have a right to know. Even this 25 year old, in this example, should be asking what his exit strategy is.

Is your financial advisor still trying to crack the code? Get one who knows it is in the Code!

What Properly Designed Life Insurance Looks Like

The properly designed life insurance contract has all the hallmarks of what the Internal Revenue Code allows when it comes to life insurance.

1. As much premium for as little death benefit as possible. If you need more on a temporary basis, purchase some term insurance to fill the gap.

2. Maximize the frequency and volume of premiums the IRC will allow. In other words, get the money in as fast as you can, but stay within the IRC rules.

3. Choose to reinvest the dividends as "paid up additions" so that they increase your cash values and your death benefits the older you get.

The properly designed life insurance contract takes advantage of all the opportunities the life insurance company will allow.

1. Payment of premium by the life insurance company in the case of your disability. You want the plan to complete itself if you can't complete it because of a disability.

2. If you can't purchase your total human life value in the form of permanent overfunded life insurance, then the policy ought to

allow you to purchase more in the future at your health today.

3. In the event of a prolonged illness, the policy ought to allow you to use an accelerated option of obtaining your death benefits.

The properly designed life insurance contract will be provided by a life insurance company that:

1. Is a mutual company, not a stock company. A mutual company exists for the benefit of the policy holders and consequently manages their profitability for the long term. A stock company exists for the benefit of the stock holders and consequently manages their profitability over the short run and the current stock price.

2. Is a "Non-direct recognition" company. This has to do with dividends. A "direct recognition" company directly recognizes loans outstanding when they grant their dividends. Policies without loans outstanding receive a greater share of the company dividend. A "non-direct recognition" company doesn't recognize outstanding loans when they grant their dividends; therefore, the company pays the same dividend regardless of any loans outstanding.

3. Sets their loan interest rate according to a well-recognized bond index. This removes the risk of excessive loan rates at the discretion of the company. Loan interest rates will be market-based, not "insurance-company-board-based."

4. Is well-rated by Standard and Poor's, A.M. Best and Moody's.

As a result, you will receive a competitive set of benefits as compared to an alternative investment that provides the same economic value.

Capital Equivalent Value

Permanent life insurance is a "hard-to-value asset." That means that its value can only be estimated when compared to the value of another asset that would provide equal benefits. The other asset could be any financial asset such as stocks, bonds, mutual funds, gold, silver, real estate, etc.

Comparing life insurance to other assets leads us back to Capital Equivalent Value. As you remember from Chapter 1, the Capital Equivalent Value of an asset was defined as the sum of money a financial asset would have to grow to in order to provide the same benefit of a another financial asset (a permanent life insurance policy in this case). Can the asset achieve the Capital Equivalent Value? If not, the permanent life policy is the better investment option.

Now, let's take a look at how to apply a Capital Equivalent Value calculation to a typical real-life scenario:

A hypothetical 55-year-old individual in good health wants to make an investment. For any number of reasons, this person is starting from scratch and needs to save at an accelerated rate in order to retire in 10 years, and they will be able to invest $100,000 per year to put toward their retirement. What is the best financial asset for them to invest in?

First, since the "hard-to-value" asset to consider is permanent life insurance, we need to identify what benefits the permanent life insurance policy in question would provide. And remember — it is more than the death benefits! A significant portion of the value of the permanent life insurance policy lies in the ability to use the cash value (the investment plus dividends) as collateral to borrow from the death benefits. In other words, the death benefits can be accessed during the lifetime of the insured without having to die, and because the cash flow from the life insurance policy will be received as a loan, it is not taxable by the Internal Revenue Service as income.

Current interest rates directly influence the interest rate a company charges for a loan and the dividends they declare. In these examples I am using 2017 interest rates.

Today a life insurance policy can provide:

- $67,000 per year ($1,675,000 total) from age 66-90, tax exempt (when taken as a loan against the death benefits).

Why 66-90? Because 66 is when social security begins for many Americans, and 90 is five years longer than normal life expectancy. We always want to plan for more life than less life!

And

A residual death benefit of:

- $1,039,000 if death at age 85 (normal life expectancy), $662,000 if death at age 90 (five years past life expectancy), or $184,000 if death at age 100 (15 years past life expectancy).

> You always want a residual death benefit when death occurs!

To summarize this investment plan:

- Total Invested: $1,000,000 (10 deposits of $100,000)
- Distributions:
  - During Life: $1,675,000 (25 loan distributions of $67,000)
  - At Death: $662,000 (death benefits at age 90)
  - Total Distributions: $2,337,000
  - Net Lifetime Gain: $1,337,000, income tax-exempt

Now that we have determined the inputs ($100,000 per year for 10 years) and outputs ($67,000 per year for 25 years plus the death benefit) of the permanent life insurance policy in question, we need to determine financial rate of distribution from the alternate investment that will provide the same outputs. This is the last number we need in order to calculate what value an alternative investment would need to achieve after 10 years in order to generate the same value that the permanent life insurance policy provides (this value is the Capital Equivalent Value).

Four percent is the generally-accepted financial rate of distribution, but that rate is actively challenged by various financial professionals. It has been derived by calculating the probability of running out of money over a lifetime. In essence, it says that there is 96% chance of running out of money before 25 years elapse from the beginning of retirement if you are invested in an evenly invested portfolio of stocks and bonds.

There are a couple of problems with the "4% rule":

1. 96% success means there is a 4% failure rate. Four out of every 100 people are going to run out of money before they run out of life. That is not bad if you are in the group of 96. However, let's say you are leaving on vacation and the pilot of your flight tells you that there is a 96% chance that your plane will land without crashing. Are you getting on that plane? I'm not!

2. The 96% success rate can mean there is as little as $1 in the nest egg 25 years from retirement. In the Capital Equivalent Value calculation, we are requiring the return of the $1,000,000 investment at life expectancy.

Rather than 4%, most Americans will settle in at somewhere between 3 and 4% as their acceptable distribution rate because at a 3% distribution rate the probability of not running out of money is closer to 100%. For my purposes in this book, we will a 3.5% distribution rate.

The general Capital Equivalent Value equation looks like this:

Life Insurance Annual Distribution divided by the Distribution Rate = Capital Equivalent Value (CEV)

In our example, the CEV of this life insurance policy is:

$67,000 / 3.5% = $1,914,285

Therefore, any other investment: stocks, bonds, mutual funds, gold, silver, real estate or ANY investment that might be invented would need to accumulate to $1,914,285 in order to provide the same level of benefits as the life insurance policy.

Capital Equivalent Value Rate of Return: The Holy Grail of Investment Gurus

I've always found it interesting that everyone wants the "best return."When they say this, they almost always are talking about a "rate of return" — a percentage. However, when you fully understand the concept of allowing your money to compound forever while using someone else's money to spend, then the volume of money is more important than the rate of return. After all, at the end of your life, when you reflect on everything you have accomplished, would you rather have had a higher rate of return or more money?

So, for those who have to have a rate of return (ROR) to feel good about an investment, the only thing left to calculate is the rate of return that is necessary for the alternate investment. That rate of return will represent what the investment has to earn in order to provide the same benefits as the life insurance contract.

Building on the example in the last chapter, the Capital Equivalent Value can be taken one step further. What would the alternate investment have to earn on an annual basis to accumulate the nest egg necessary to provide the same benefits of the hard-to-value investment.In this case, the permanent life insurance policy. This is the Capital Equivalent Value Rate of Return (CEV ROR).

The calculation is fairly simple:

$100,000 per year for 10 years must grow to $1,914,285. (CEV)

The rate necessary to achieve that growth is 11.54%. (CEV ROR)

Because the life insurance proceeds are tax-exempt, the $67,000 from the alternative investment must also be tax-exempt. This means that the Capital Equivalent Value must be grossed up for the taxes that would be due and the Capital Equivalent Value Rate of Return must be recalculated for each tax bracket:

Income Tax Bracket	CEV	CEV Rate of Return
15%	$2,252,100	14.37%
25%	$2,552,380	16.55%
40%	$3,190,475	20.41%

What about investment fees?

The values and rates of return above that were adjusted for the tax-exempt nature of the permanent life insurance contract must be increased again if there are any investment fees associated with the alternative investment. The values from the life insurance contract are from after all fees and expenses are accounted for.

How often do these rates of return need to be realized? Can they fluctuate? Can't we just use average rates of return over time?

These rates of return must be realized every year for 10 years without fail. You can't earn less of what is required one year and make it up the next. It won't work. Why?

Assume an investment balance of $10,000 that grows 10% each year for 2 years. At the end of 2 years you would have $12,100.

If that same investment balance would grow at 5% one of the years and 15% the other (still a 10% average annual rate of return), the account balance would only be $12,075.

Any deviance from the average always results in less money.

The rate must stay the same every year for 10 years without fail!

Life Insurance Trickle-Down Effect: Social Security

What are the unexpected benefits of tax-exempt withdrawals?

Today, in general, 50% of your social security is taxable at your highest income tax bracket rate if your "provisional" income exceeds $25,000 (if you are single) or $32,000 (if you are married).

Today, as much as 85% of your social security payments could be subject to this additional income tax at higher thresholds of "provisional income."

"Provisional" income is your gross income plus 50% of your gross social security payments, plus your tax-free interest. That's right — your tax free municipal bond interest may make your social security taxable. So much for tax free! There is a difference between tax free and tax exempt.

We now see that anything tax free is still reported to the US Government for "tax purposes". In this case, to determine the taxability of your social security. What other tax-free investments are reported to the US Government for "tax purposes"? A distribution from your Roth IRA is reported on a 1099R form, even though it is not taxable income. Will it ever be included as taxable income? Will it ever become part of the "provisional income" definition? We don't know, but it is being reported.

To make matters worse — haven't you already been taxed on your social security deposits when you were working? Of course you were. Our taxable income is determined when social security taxes are withheld. If they are taxed again when you receive the benefits, that would be double taxation. If your Members of Congress know about this double taxation, that means that your interests were represented when this second tax was enacted in 1984. We started a revolution in this country because we were being taxed once by the British government without representation! Now, this is double taxation with representation! Isn't it time you did something about this? You can. Live your retirement years without having reportable taxable or provisional income.

What does this mean for the Capital Equivalent Value and Capital Equivalent Value Rate of Return calculations?

Today, in 2018, the maximum someone can receive in social security benefits at normal retirement age is $33,456 per year. The non-working marriage partner of that recipient would be entitled to a minimum of $16,728 per year for a total of $50,184 (although working spouses are entitled to 100% of their earned social security which may exceed the 50% of a non-working spouse).

One half of the $50,184 is what is automatically added to "provisional" income. That is $25,092. That doesn't even leave $7,000 from other sources before any social security is taxed. If your "provisional income" is $31,999, none of your social security is taxed. If your "provisional income" is $32,000 (just one dollar more), then your social security begins to be taxed. Up to 85%

of social security is taxed for a married couple beginning at $44,000 of provisional income. That only leaves $18,908 for municipal bond income and distributions from your 401(k) and IRAs before the maximum percentage of social security is subject to taxation.

If 85% of the social security is taxed, that will add $42,656 ($50,184 x 85%) of taxable income to this retiree's tax return.In the following tax brackets, that means this couple will be paying more income tax. For most who read this, this is likely something you did not know:

Income Tax Bracket	Additional Tax
15%	$6,398
25%	$10,664
40%	$17,062

If you are retired for 25 years (ages 66-90) you could have to pay the following taxes that you would not have to pay if you had utilized the Internal Revenue Code to your advantage:

Income Tax Bracket	Additional Tax	25 Years of Additional Tax
15%	$6,398	$159,950
25%	$10,664	$266,600
40%	$17,062	$426,550

Now that you know the truth, how does that make you feel? Are you ready to do something about it?

Because loan proceeds from a life insurance contract are not considered either taxable or provisional income, the life insurance distribution in the example two chapters earlier of $67,000 a year is tax-exempt and will not cause your social security to be taxable.If your life insurance distribution is able to keep you under the social security taxability thresholds, your life insurance has just added more money to your pocketbook, represented by the taxes you don't have to pay!

To get a fair representation of what your life insurance contract is now worth, you have to recalculate the Capital Equivalent Value and its Rate of Return.

To determine the Capital Equivalent Value and the Capital Equivalent Value Rate of Return while taking into account the tax effect of social security, you must add the additional tax to the required distribution from the alternative investment. If your alternate investment causes your social security to be taxable, you must withdraw the taxes due on the social security from the alternative investment cash flow to make the comparison to life insurance legitimate. The distribution from the alternative investment taking this into account is no longer $67,000, but rather:

Tax Bracket	Required Distribution Amount (RDA)
15%	$73,398
25%	$77,664
40%	$84,062

Now that the required distribution amounts are different, the Capital Equivalent Value and the Capital Equivalent Value Rate of Return have to be recalculated. Using the same calculation as described earlier, the CEV and CEV ROR are:

Tax Bracket	RDA	CEV	CEV ROR
15%	$73,398	$2,097,085	13.13%
25%	$77,664	$2,218,971	14.11%
40%	$84,062	$2,401,771	15.49%

Remembering that life insurance proceeds are tax exempt, we need to adjust the CEV numbers because they need to reflect an after-tax balance so that we can distribute an after-tax amount.

Tax Bracket	RDA	Before tax CEV	Before Tax CEV ROR
15%	$73,167	$2,467,158	15.96%
25%	$77,278	$2,958,628	19.11%
40%	$83,444	$4,002,951	24.35%

These values and Rates of Return must be increased if there are any investment fees associated with the alternative investment.

These Rates of Return must be realized every year for 10 years without fail.

Every year for 10 years without fail!

Let's Recap:

You start with $100,000 per year to invest for 10 years beginning at age 55. The permanent life insurance policy will make it spend as if it were $4,000,000 after your accumulation period, over your lifetime.

Has your financial advisor ever explained this to you before?

Hopefully you now understand why an asset distribution plan is more important than an asset accumulation plan.

What if you only had $80,000 per year to "invest" for 10 years? By focusing on asset distribution, you may have more spendable cash flow in your retirement years than if you had invested $100,000 per year with the investments that are only focused on accumulation. Getting to the top of Mount Everest may not be in your best interest.

Life Insurance Trickle-Down Effect: Medicare and Other Income-Based Benefits

Did you know that not everyone pays the same Medicare premium at age 65?

The amount you pay is determined by your income the two years before the current year. The more "income" you report on your income tax return the more you pay for Medicare.

"Income" refers to your 401(k), Pension, IRA distributions, up to 85% of your social security benefits, any other taxable income you may have, plus your tax-exempt interest income. The federal government has not yet required that your Roth IRA distributions be included in your Modified Adjusted Gross Income (MAGI).

Everyone in 2018 paid at least $134 per month for Part B Medicare, but you could have been required to pay as much as $428 per month for the same set of benefits. That is potentially $3,528 more per year if your alternative investment is taxable income. Since life insurance is tax-exempt, that is another adjustment you must make to the CEV and CEV Rate of Return calculations.

What about other income-based benefits?

They think of new ones every year!The more income you have, the less you get. If you don't have "income," then you get ALL of the benefits.

Conclusion

In 2018, it is time for some new financial metrics!

For as long as I can remember – and that has been forty years as a CPA – financial professionals have depended on the same few financial measurements. A mainstay of these financial metrics is "rate of return." In fact, many other financial measurements include "rate of return" as one of their measurement parameters or givens. But are these measurements enough to assess all of the variables we are looking to measure today?

In the baseball world, the measurement of success or progress used to be measured by just a few metrics, too. Growing up, I remember that the only thing that mattered was a pitcher's earned run average (ERA), a batter's batting average, a batter's runs batted in (RBI), and a fielder's number of errors made.

Today, times have changed. Baseball is more competitive than ever, and the metrics have evolved to measure an increasing number of variables that determine a player's success.

- Pitchers are now measured by: APP, BK, BF, BS, CG, ER, ERA, AO, GF, GS, GO, HLD, IR, IP, I, K, NP, PK, QS, RW, SV, SVO, SV%, SHO, SO, UER, WHIP, WP, W, and WPCT.

- Hitters are measured by: AB, AVG, CS, 2B, XBH, G, GSH, GIDP, GO/AO, HBP, H, HR, IBB,

> LOB, OBP, OPS, PA, ROE, R, RBI, SH, SF, 1B, SLG, SB, SB%, TB, 3B, BB, and WO.

- Fielders are now measured by: A, CS%, DP, E, FPCT, INN, O, OFA, PB, PO, TC, and TP. (source: MLB.com standard stats)

Wow, that's quite an evolution!

If the sports world has refined and improved their methods of measuring success over time, isn't it time for the financial world to do the same?

In the financial world, the rate of return has typically only measured the return over a long period of time. But today, you now understand that financial accumulation years does not necessarily define the best financial distribution during retirement years. Success cannot only be measured by simply calculating the rate of return over that entire period of time. We need new financial metrics for this task!

Capital Equivalent Value (CEV) and Capital Equivalent Value Rate of Return (CEV ROR) are the new financial metrics that achieve this calculation goal.

It has taken four years to write this book as it has grown from the inception of the idea in a small conference room at a hotel in Franklin, Tennessee, to what I hope becomes a new hallmark of financial success. Along the way, these ideas and calculations have been reviewed and challenged by countless financial professionals until we determined we had true and accurate measurements. CEV and CEV ROR are refining measurements of financial success, just as a baseball pitcher's walks and hits per inning pitched (WHIP) further defines the effectiveness of a baseball pitcher beyond ERA.

CEV and CEV ROR give the ability to accurately determine value that was previously unable to be measured in the financial world. My hope is that this new understanding will give you further tools to achieve greater personal and professional financial success.

Afterword

I am honored that I was asked to write this afterword. I have been an insurance and financial professional for over 15 years and have known Bryan as a mentor and a great friend to myself and my family for eight of those years. Bryan and I have common concerns about the industry and the pitfalls associated with traditional financial planning.

Bryan is well regarded and well respected in our industry. I applaud him for taking the steps – and the journey – that he's been on with regard to challenging conventional thinking, developing his personal motivations and beliefs, and his boundless enthusiasm and willingness to share this knowledge.

The strategy Bryan communicates requires that he courageously swim upstream – to continually challenge, educate, and engage others about something they deserve to know and understand. He remains a forward thinker in his commitment to take this stand, especially as a CPA. He is a tireless advocate for helping people learn the truth about money and how it really works. It's easy to do what everyone else is doing – however, the truth will set you free; and Bryan considers it his mission to share the truth about wealth.

This book is yet another example of the way we verify and prove how money really works. It is truly about distribution – as that is the only real reason anyone saves for retirement. Yet the industry as a whole is focused on accumulation. In traditional financial planning, what we see is that people have no exit strategy for retirement. They are simply stuck. Bryan helps shift the focus from the government and financial institutions that are winning every day back to the people.

John Dwyer

I am so glad Bryan has taken the time to clearly articulate where your money rests is by far more important than its potential rate of return.

Sixty-two percent of Americans could literally stop filing income tax returns during retirement based on our 105 year old tax code, if they simply knew what we know.

Thank you Bryan for the truth!

Tom Love

About Bryan S. Bloom, CPA

Bryan began his financial career immediately following earning his CPA credentials and Bachelor's Degree in Accountancy from the University of Illinois. Later he earned his Master's Degree in Business Administration from the University of Illinois Executive MBA program.

His career started as a staff accountant for the State Universities Retirement System of Illinois where he eventually became the Chief Financial Officer. After 19 years of experience in public retirement matters, he worked for 5 years with Benefit Planning Consultants, Inc. - a third party administration corporation overseeing private retirement plans.

He is currently associated with The America Group, and he has been assisting individuals in their personal retirement planning for the last 18 years.

Bryan earned Million Dollar Round Table membership within four months in the personal financial industry in 2000. He earned VIP of the Year award from Ohio National Financial Services that same year. In 2010, Bryan was recognized by Ohio National with their Chairman's Navigator Award, recognizing him for the personal integrity Bryan exhibits with his clients and business relationships.

Bryan and his spouse of 36 years, Pam, live in Champaign, Illinois. They have two daughters, Callie and Corrie and three grandchildren, Emmie, Ellie and Coen.

You can contact Bryan at
bbloom@theamericagroup.com

"Discovery is seeing what everybody else has seen, and thinking what nobody else has thought."

Dr. Albert Szent-Györgyi, Nobel Prize Winner

What are your observations?

CPSIA information can be obtained
at www.ICGtesting.com
Printed in the USA
FSHW01n1219180518
48161FS